Technology All Around Us

Medicine

Dr K R Routh

W

FRANKLIN WATTS

LONDON•SYDNEY

First published in 2005 by
Franklin Watts
96 Leonard Street
London EC2A 4XD

Franklin Watts Australia
Level 17/207 Kent Street
Sydney
NSW 2000

Produced by Arcturus Publishing Ltd,
26/27 Bickels Yard, 151-153 Bermondsey Street,
London SE1 3HA

© 2005 Arcturus Publishing

Series concept: Alex Woolf
Editor: Alex Woolf
Designer: Simon Borrough
Picture researcher: Glass Onion Pictures

Picture Credits:
Science Photo Library: 4 (Richard T. Nowitz), 5 (Simon Fraser),
6 (Mark Thomas), 7 (Alfred Pasieka), 8 (Saturn Stills), 9
(Zephyr), 10 (John Greim), 11 (David M. Martin, M.D.), 12
(Antonia Reeve), 13 (Antonia Reeve), 14 (Chris Priest), 15
(John Bavosi), 16 (Catherine Ursillo), 17 (James King-Holmes),
18 (Du Cane Medical Imaging Ltd), 19 (Ouellette & Theroux,
Publiphoto Diffusion), 21 (Hank Morgan), 22 (Deep Light
Productions), 24 (Siu), 25 (Antonia Reeve), 26 (Horacio
Sormani), 27 (David Nunuk), 28 and cover (NIH/Custom
Medical Stock Photo), 29 (John Bavosi).
Topham Picturepoint: 23 (Richard Ellis/The Image Works).

Every attempt has been made to clear copyright. Should there
be any inadvertent omission, please apply to the publisher for
rectification.

A CIP catalogue record for this book is available from the British
Library.

ISBN 0 7496 5958 0

Printed in Singapore

Contents

Technology plays a very important role in medicine. Machines are used every day to find out what's wrong when someone is ill, to do the work of worn out or damaged body parts and even to keep people alive.

Seeing Into the Body

Machines can look inside the body without having to cut the skin. X-ray machines, ultrasound and medical scanners take pictures of our bones, internal organs and blood vessels.

Tiny cameras on long tubes and in capsules can go inside the body to look for problems in the gut and other body parts. Technology like this helps the doctor to decide what is wrong, and what treatment is needed.

Looking Forward

Digital Doctors Complex computer programs are being written that can help decide what is wrong with a patient. The patient answers questions put by the computer which then makes a likely diagnosis.

One day these computers may be able to diagnose illnesses on their own, but most patients will probably still want to see a human doctor when they are ill.

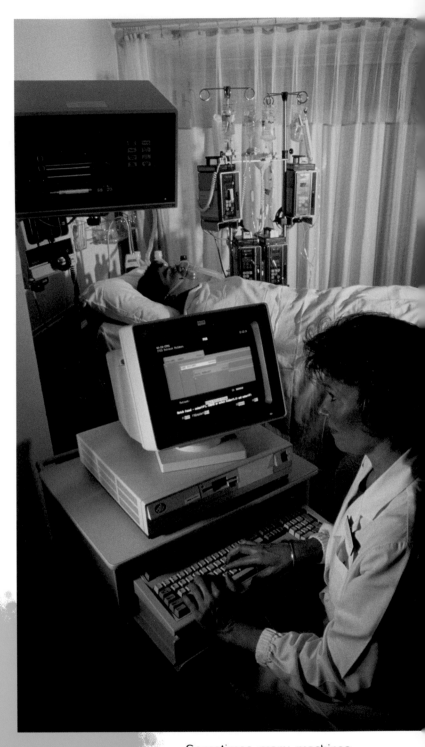

Sometimes many machines are needed to help look after patients, such as here in an intensive care ward.

Helping the Body to Work

From hearing aids to artificial legs, technology can be used to help or replace lots of different functions of the body.

Artificial hearts can boost the strength of a failing human heart, and dialysis machines do the work of damaged kidneys. Without these man-made organs, many people would lead a much poorer life.

Some technology provides "life support" – without them a person would die. Ventilators and heart-lung machines perform the vital roles of breathing and pumping blood. Tiny babies are kept alive in high-tech incubators which monitor their every move.

Humans still Needed

Technology is important in modern medicine, but it will never replace the skills and care of our healthcare workers. Machines cannot offer the human contact we need when we are very ill.

Although stethoscopes have been around for nearly two hundred years, they are still used by healthcare staff around the world every day.

The Stethoscope Doctors and nurses have been using special medical tools for many years. The stethoscope has been used to listen to the heart and lungs since its invention in 1816 by Laennec, a French doctor.

Although there are newer, more complicated ways to do this now, the stethoscope is still used by doctors in hospitals all over the world.

5

Looking Inside the Body

When a person becomes ill, doctors use X-ray machines and body scanners to "look" inside the body to see what the problem is.

Looking Back

X-rays were discovered in 1895 by the German physicist Wilhelm Roentgen. He took an X-ray picture of his wife's hand, and newspapers around the world reported the news of his find.

Doctors soon realized how useful these new pictures could be for finding broken bones and even lost bullets.

The doughnut-shaped **CAT** scanner uses computers to make pictures of the inside of the patient's body.

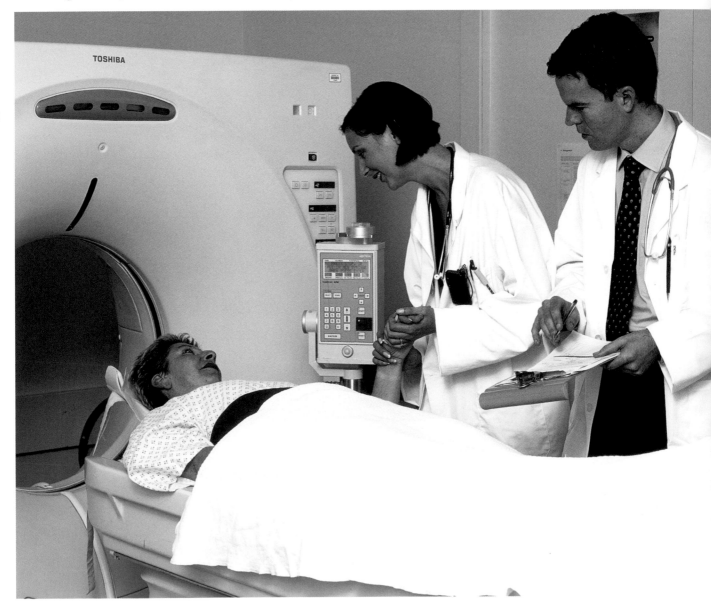

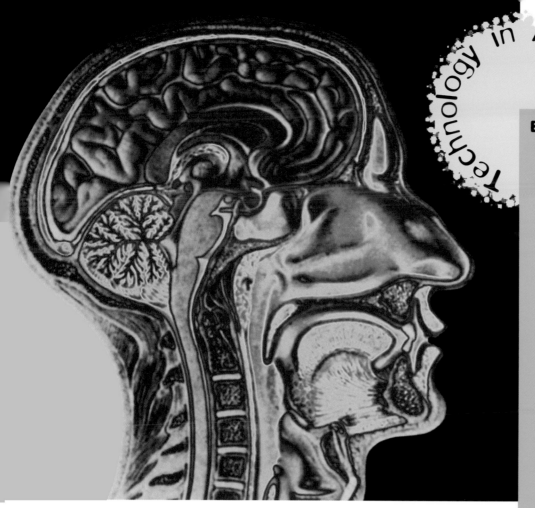

Scans, like this MRI (Magnetic Resonance Imaging) scan of a healthy head, can show great detail inside the body.

Brain Scan

Little Sara was just seventeen months old when her mum became worried that she was not holding her head up properly. It was decided that she should have a special test called an MRI scan to look inside her head.

The doctors were surprised to find a tumour (lump) inside which was pressing on her brain. She needed an operation to remove it. Luckily it wasn't the kind of tumour which is really harmful and grows back, so the doctors think she will be fine now.

X-ray Machines

An X-ray machine is rather like a camera but, unlike normal photographs, X-ray pictures show the inside of the body.

When an X-ray picture is held up to a strong light, bones appear white, and air-filled spaces (like the lungs) appear black. Soft tissues like the heart and intestines appear grey.

X-ray pictures are useful for finding broken bones and looking for diseases such as cancer or infection. And if you accidentally swallow a solid object, an X-ray can be used to find out where it has gone.

Body Scanners

Sometimes doctors need to see inside the body in great detail. This is when body scanners may be used – large, complicated machines which use fast computers. The pictures they produce look like slices of the body and show the internal parts quite clearly. You may have heard of one type – the CAT scanner. (CAT stands for computerized axial tomography.)

The person having the scan lies on a bed which then moves inside the doughnut-shaped scanner. It is a bit noisy but it doesn't hurt.

Body scanners can show if there is disease or damage in any part of the body. These scans cost a lot of money (much more than most X-rays), so they are only used if really necessary.

Bats and dolphins use sound waves to find out what is around them. We can use sound in a similar way to "see" inside the body. This way of looking inside the body is called ultrasound scanning. It is very safe and widely used.

The ultrasound machine has a part called a probe which looks rather like a microphone. Placed against the skin, it sends sound waves into the part of the body being studied. These bounce back to form a picture which appears on a monitor. The monitor shows a moving image, like a video, from which snapshots can be taken.

Looking Forward

Virtual Reality In the future, surgeons may be able to operate inside the body by using computer-generated "virtual" images provided by ultrasound. The surgeon will wear a headset and will see himself doing the operation as though he is playing a video or computer game.

Seeing Unborn Babies

Ultrasound is used to find out whether a baby is growing well inside its mother. Most pregnant women have at least one ultrasound scan. It is quite safe for the baby and the mother. The tiny, growing baby can be seen many months before it is born. Its heart and other parts can be checked and measured. Sometimes you can even tell if it is a boy or a girl.

This pregnant woman is having an ultrasound scan. Her unborn baby can be seen on the monitors.

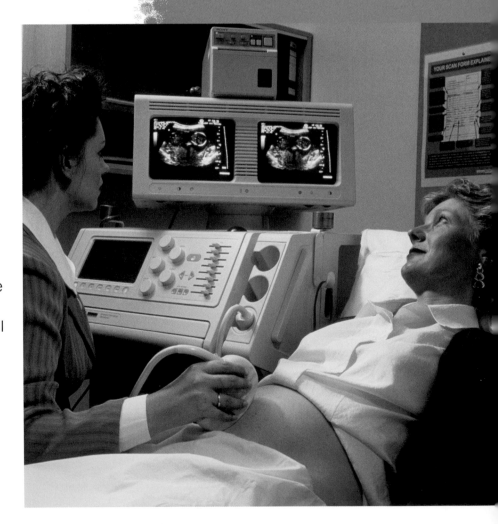

Watching Blood Moving

This ultrasound scan shows blood slowing down because of a blockage in an artery (slow-moving blood shows as green; faster blood shows up red).

Ultrasound is also used to study the way blood flows through the heart and around the body. If an artery is blocked by a blood clot, the blood will stop flowing through it. An ultrasound scan can show this and so help the surgeon to decide whether an operation is needed to unblock the artery.

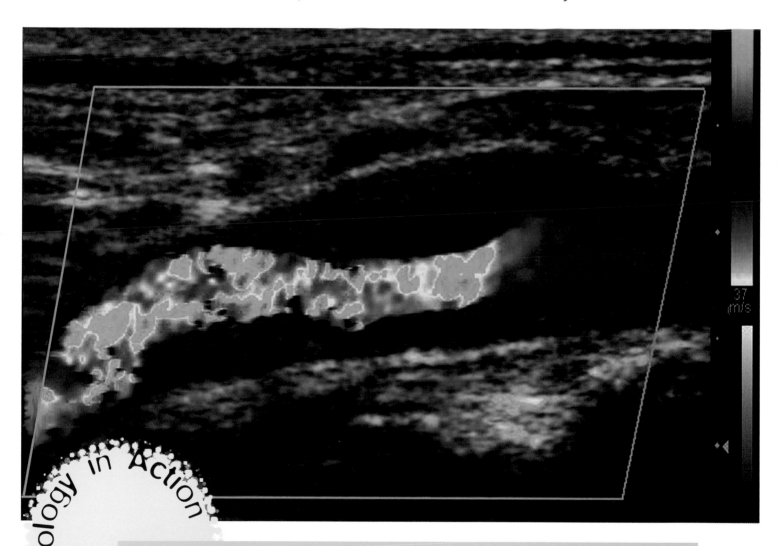

Ultrasound Test

It's January 2001, in the UK, and Jenny Moss is having a test called an echocardiogram. This test uses ultrasound to look closely at the heart and the way blood flows through it.

Jenny is having this test because her doctor heard a murmur (an abnormal heart sound) when he listened to her chest. He was worried that she might have a damaged heart. Luckily, the test shows that everything is fine.

Tiny Cameras

If you want to take a picture of the inside of your mouth, you could do it with an ordinary camera. But imagine that you need a picture of further down, inside your stomach. You would need a very tiny camera, and it would need to be on the end of a long, bendy tube.

Doctors use an endoscope to look down inside a patient's nose. The endoscope sends pictures to the monitor behind them.

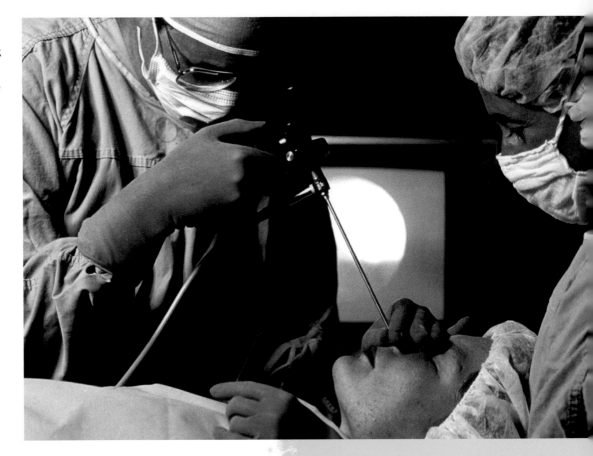

Endoscopes

There are cameras like this, called endoscopes. In medicine they are used in many ways. Some go down through the mouth into the gullet, stomach or lungs.

Some go up the other way, through the bottom, to look at the intestines. And some are used during operations where they are pushed through tiny cuts in the skin while the patient is asleep.

Doctors look at the pictures sent back by the endoscopes to see if there are any areas of disease or damage. Sometimes they use a tiny tool in the endoscope to take a sample of tissue away to look at it more closely under the microscope.

Looking Back

Limited Vision Before we had endoscopes, doctors called to see a sick patient could only see into the body a short way. They couldn't look round corners. For example, a doctor could look into your mouth to see a sore throat, but could not look further down into the stomach to see an ulcer.

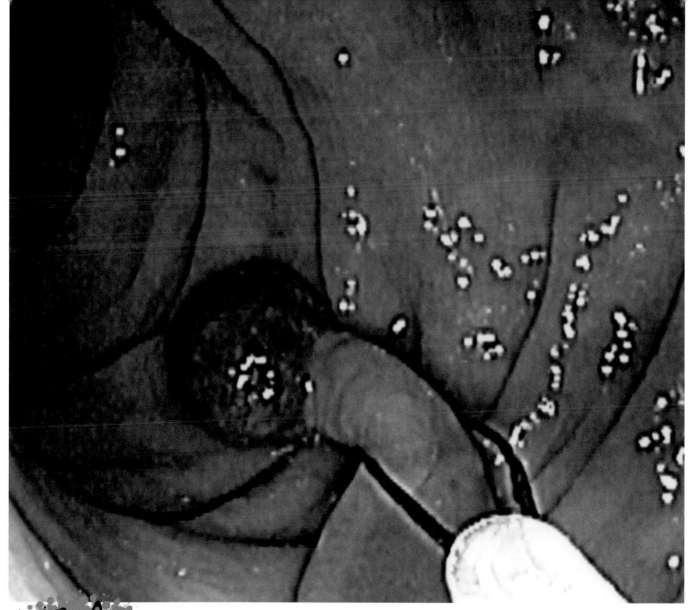

This picture from an endoscope shows a small growth, called a polyp, being removed from inside the intestine by using a loop of sharp wire.

View from the Inside
Samuel, 65, has been having strange stomach aches and diarrhoea for many years until his doctor decides to try the new capsule camera on him.

Sam finds the test simple and painless. The pictures taken by the camera show that he has a disease of the intestine called Crohn's. Now he is on the right treatment and is doing well.

The Camera Pill
Endoscopes have a problem: they aren't long enough or bendy enough to go all the way down inside the intestines. So scientists invented the capsule camera – a camera in the form of a large pill.

The patient swallows the "pill" and it takes pictures as it goes right through the hard-to-reach parts of the intestines, and out the other end.

In the past, when surgeons wanted to do an operation, they would have to make a large cut in the skin to be able to see and work inside the body. These long cuts – perhaps five to ten centimetres or more – are then stitched up and take several weeks to heal.

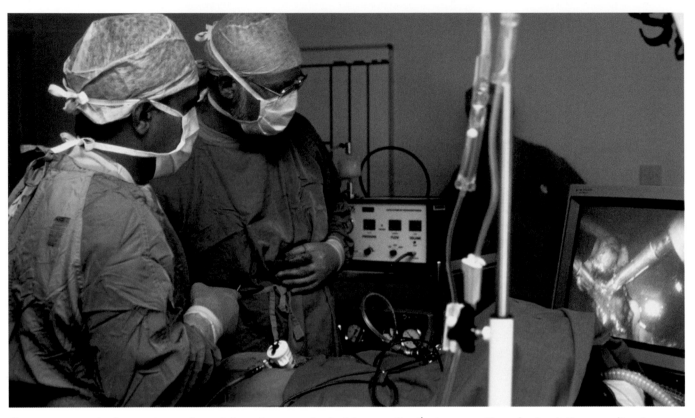

Surgeons use instruments on long tubes to operate inside a patient's tummy. They look at the monitor to see what is going on inside as they work.

Today, many operations can be done through tiny cuts, perhaps only one or two centimetres long. This has become known as keyhole surgery. In these operations the surgeon usually makes several small cuts, just large enough to allow the special surgical instruments through.

Keyhole surgery is changing the way our hospitals and surgeons work. Smaller surgical wounds mean that patients get better more quickly. They are also less likely to get an infection. Their hospital stay is usually shorter, with many going home the same day.

Looking Forward

Remote Control It is likely that an increasing number of different types of operation will be done by keyhole surgery in the future.

Medical scientists are now working on ways to perform these operations by remote control, as many of the tiny instruments employed are tricky to work with using the human hand.

The Surgical Instruments

The surgeon uses several different types of instrument to do keyhole surgery. To see what is going on inside the body he uses an endoscope, a tube with a camera at the end (see pages 10–11).

Then, depending on the type of operation, he uses other tiny instruments which cut tissue, hold internal organs or clip off blood vessels. Each of these instruments is at the end of a long tube which is pushed through a small cut in the skin.

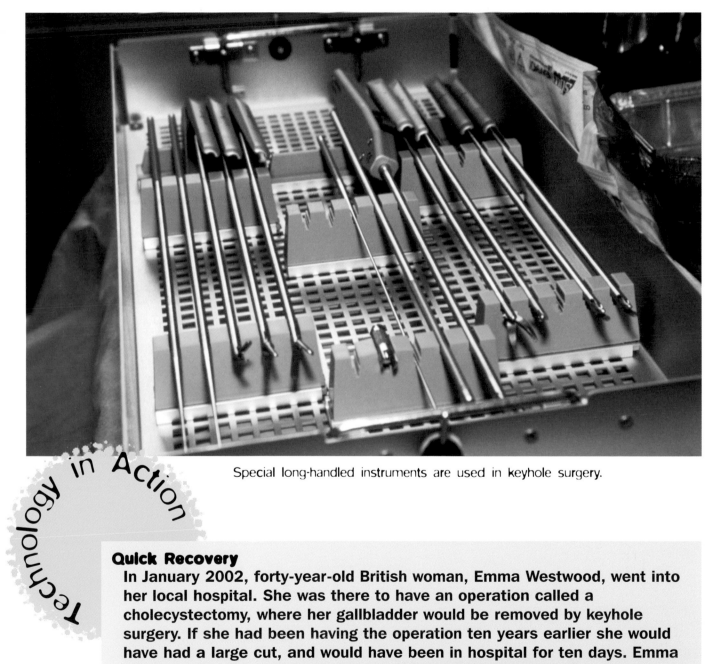

Special long-handled instruments are used in keyhole surgery.

Technology in Action

Quick Recovery

In January 2002, forty-year-old British woman, Emma Westwood, went into her local hospital. She was there to have an operation called a cholecystectomy, where her gallbladder would be removed by keyhole surgery. If she had been having the operation ten years earlier she would have had a large cut, and would have been in hospital for ten days. Emma felt fine after the operation and left the hospital the same day. She was back at work four weeks later.

Most of us take our ears for granted, but some people need the help of technology to enable them to hear.

Hearing Aids

Many people who are hard-of-hearing use hearing aids. A hearing aid is a battery-operated electronic device which receives sound through a microphone. It then amplifies this sound (makes it louder) and sends it to the ear through a tiny speaker.

Hearing aids only work if the person can still hear sounds. They will not work for someone who is completely deaf.

There are several different kinds of hearing aid. In one of the most common types, the main part of the device tucks behind the ear and there is a plastic part which fits into the hole of the ear.

Looking Back

Ear Trumpets Invented in the 1800s, the first hearing aids were known as ear trumpets. They were made of various materials including silver and tortoiseshell.

These were not electronic devices. They were really just like large funnels which people spoke into so that the user could hear what was being said.

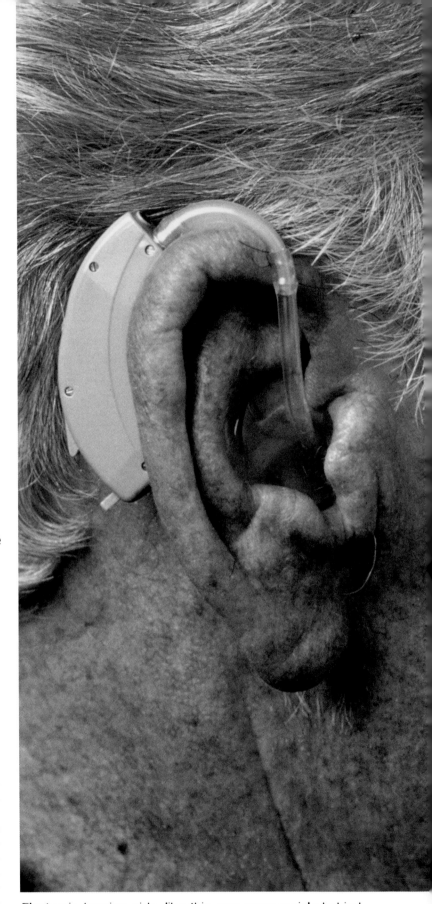

Electronic hearing aids, like this one worn mainly behind the ear, are made up of a microphone, an amplifier and a tiny speaker.

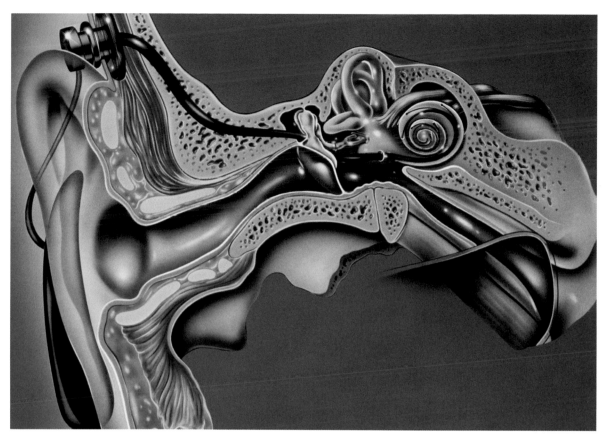

This cutaway picture shows how a cochlear implant fits inside the ear.

Cochlear Implants

If someone is deaf or extremely hard-of-hearing they may be given a different electronic device called a cochlear implant. These are named after the cochlea, the part of the inside of the ear which turns sound waves into nerve signals to send to the brain.

A cochlear implant is a tiny machine which tries to do the job of the real cochlea when that part of the ear is not working properly. The device has some parts which are implanted under the skin behind the ear in a surgical operation, and some parts which are worn on a belt or in a pocket.

New Sounds

Jake, aged fifteen, had worn hearing aids for many years, but had always been able to hear a little. Then one day he found he couldn't hear anything at all. His doctors suggested that a cochlear implant might help, and the operation was carried out in January 2004.

At first Jake didn't like it. Everything sounded too different. But he soon got used to the implant and now his parents say he is "like a new kid".

Replacing Lost Limbs

Artificial limbs can allow people to carry on with their normal lives – and even achieve sporting success.

Fighting Back

When US athlete John Register lost his lower left leg in an accident during training in 1994, it looked like his career in sports was over. But John was determined to compete again.

With the help of a specially designed artificial leg, he soon began training in the sprint and long jump. He went on to get the silver medal in the long jump in the Sydney 2000 Paralympics.

Imagine what it would be like to be without an arm or a leg. People can lose a limb through an accident, cancer or even a war injury. Some children are born without a limb, or with one which has not grown properly.

No man-made limb can ever be as good as the real thing. But modern artificial arms and legs can help give their users an almost normal lifestyle.

The man-made limbs – also called limb prostheses – are made from a mixture of materials, including plastic, metal and foam rubber. New lightweight materials like Kevlar, carbon fibre and titanium are helping to make artificial limbs stronger and lighter.

Where there is a joint – for instance at the elbow or the knee – the limbs are designed to bend in the same way as the real joint.

Movement of the limb can be "mechanical", where the person's own muscle power moves it through a series of cables.

Or movement can be "electronic", where the power comes from a battery. Sometimes both methods are used.

Special Features

There are many types of artificial limbs, with some being designed for different activities. For example, there are sports limbs with special features which allow the person to run faster, or throw and catch a tennis ball.

There are even "swimming" legs which have holes to allow water to fill them so that they don't float too much.

Looking Forward

Thought Power Some scientists believe that one day there will be artificial limbs which can work by thought alone. Special sensors will be connected to the brain which can send messages directly to the man-made limb.

This is very similar to the way our nerves work, and would be a great breakthrough in making these limbs as real as possible.

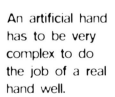

An artificial hand has to be very complex to do the job of a real hand well.

The heart is a large muscle which beats around seventy times every minute, every day of our lives. There is a special area of heart muscle called a pacemaker which tells the rest of the muscle how often to contract.

Mechanical Pacemakers

If the heart's own pacemaker doesn't work properly a mechanical pacemaker might be used. This is a small, battery-operated electronic device which is implanted under the skin in a patient's chest. It has wires which go to the heart to check how often the heart is beating.

If the heart goes too slowly the pacemaker sends an electrical signal down the wires which makes the heart muscle contract.

This coloured X-ray shows a surgically implanted heart pacemaker.

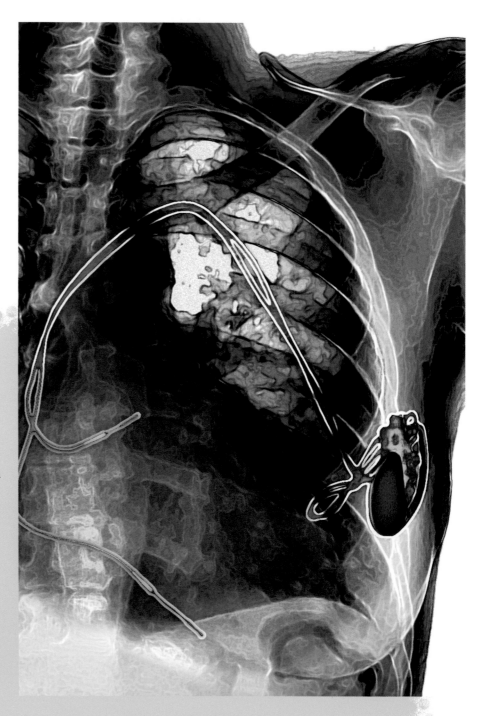

Looking Back

The First Pacemaker The first mechanical pacemaker was invented in 1950, but it wasn't until 1958 that a team of Swedish doctors implanted one inside a human body. The patient died after three hours.

The next year an American doctor, Wilson Greatbach, was more successful. The pacemaker he developed kept one of his patients alive for eighteen months.

Defibrillators

You have probably seen a defibrillator being used in medical dramas on TV. The doctor holds a "paddle" in each hand, shouts "stand clear", then presses the paddles to the patient's chest and gives an electric shock.

What is happening is that the patient's heart muscle has suddenly started to quiver, or fibrillate, instead of contracting properly. No blood gets pumped and the patient will die unless a proper heartbeat can be started soon.

The paddles send an electrical impulse through the heart which makes the heart muscle contract properly. The doctor makes everyone stand back so that they won't get a jolt of electricity, too.

A monitor screen shows the heart's electrical activity so the doctor can see how well the heart has responded.

Looking Forward

On-the-Spot Treatment New "semi-automatic" defibrillators are designed to offer step-by-step instructions to the person using them. Ambulance personnel, fire-fighters and police officers are among the people who can be trained to use these machines.

In the future these defibrillators may be available in public places so that people who need this lifesaving treatment can be helped right away.

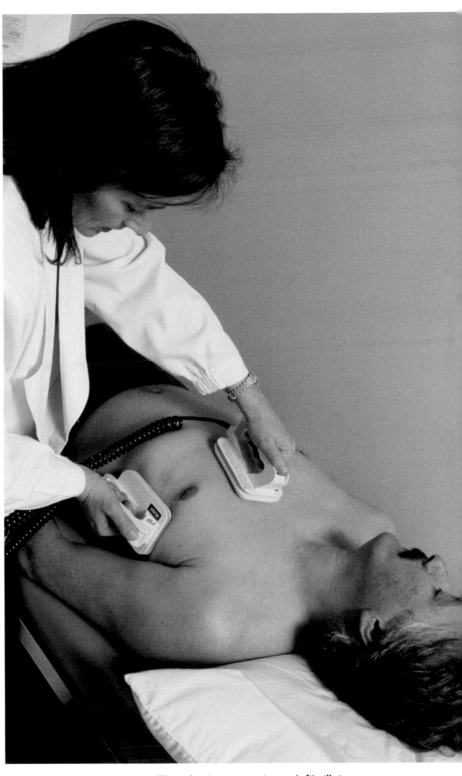

The doctor uses two defibrillator paddles, sending an electric shock to make the heart beat properly again.

19

Mechanical Hearts

Sometimes, because of disease, the heart becomes too weak to do its job properly. Then a heart transplant is needed. A donor heart is taken from someone who has recently died.

Sadly there are never enough donor hearts, so medical scientists have developed machines which can do the work of the heart, at least for a while.

Helping the Heart

Sometimes the heart can still pump, but it needs a bit of extra help. Left ventricular assist devices (LVADs) are machines which work together with the person's own heart.

In the past LVADs were large machines used only in hospitals. Newer, smaller models are now being used which can be put inside the body so the person can walk around and live fairly normally.

One type is the Jarvik 2000, which is a tiny, battery-operated turbine (a bit like a jet engine). This is put inside the heart and helps to push the blood through. The batteries are usually recharged through a socket in the skin behind the ear.

Looking Forward

From Living Tissue Mechanical devices to help or replace the heart are improving, but many people think there is a better option – hearts made from living tissue grown in laboratories.

This may seem like science fiction, but it could happen. And these living hearts could have far fewer problems than their mechanical cousins.

Dr Robert Jarvik (left), inventor of the Jarvik 2000, holds his invention near the chest of Peter Houghton, the first patient to receive the LVAD in June 2000.

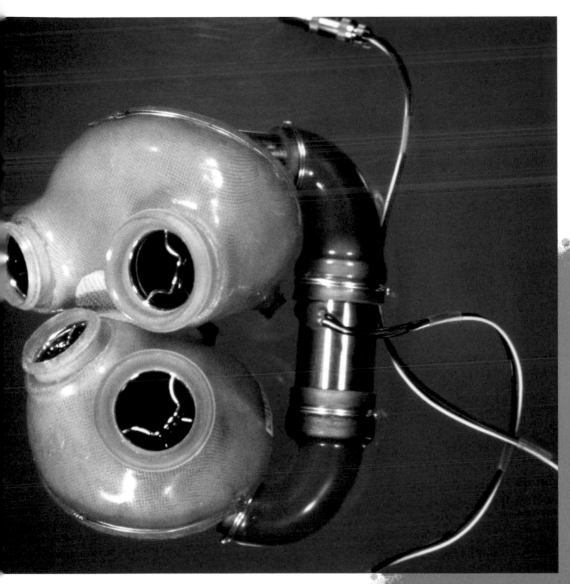

The Jarvik 7, an artificial heart made of aluminium and plastic, was used in the first human implant in 1982.

Replacing a Heart

Replacing the heart completely has been less successful. For many years scientists have been trying to make an artificial heart which is safe and works well.

One of the biggest problems is that man-made materials tend to make the blood form clots (solid lumps) which can then block important blood vessels.

One artificial heart being developed in the US is known as the Abiocor. Hopefully, one day, this type of heart may help many people who would otherwise die of heart failure.

Looking Back

Artificial Hearts The earliest artificial hearts were tested in animals in the 1950s. In 1969 the Texas Heart Institute successfully kept a patient alive for sixty hours with their version.

And in 1982, in Utah, a patient named Barney Clark was given an artificial heart (the Jarvik 7) and became famous for being kept alive for 112 days.

To stay alive the body needs to take in oxygen and send it around the body in the bloodstream. Normally the lungs and heart do this, but sometimes the body needs the help of machines.

Breathing Machines

Sometimes patients are not able to breathe for themselves. This may be after an accident, or because they are unconscious for a surgical operation. There are machines called ventilators which can help them breathe.

The ventilator pushes a mixture of air and pure oxygen down through a tube into the patient's lungs. This is done in regular "breaths" several times a minute.

Ventilators have lots of different monitors and alarms which tell the healthcare staff if something is wrong with the patient or the machine. This is important because the patient needs the machine to stay alive.

Bypassing the Heart and Lungs

A surgeon may need to operate on the heart and this cannot be done if the heart muscle is moving. So a cardiopulmonary bypass, or heart-lung machine, is used.

This machine has long tubes which collect blood as it first arrives at the heart. The blood is then sent through the heart-lung machine, which loads it with oxygen and then pumps it back into the main artery of the body, the aorta.

Because the machine does the pumping, the heart muscle can be made to stop beating for the operation.

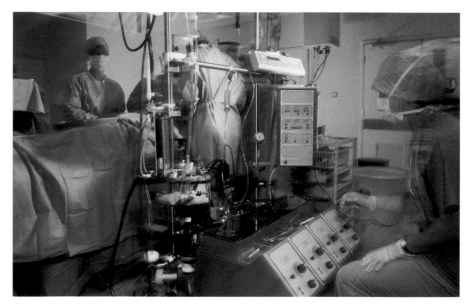

The complicated heart-lung machine does the work of the heart while doctors operate on that organ.

Looking Back

Iron Lungs Before a vaccine was discovered in 1955, a viral disease called polio affected millions of people, leaving many unable to breathe on their own. These people had to spend weeks or months living in large, coffin-shaped ventilator machines called iron lungs. Photographs from the time show whole wards of these iron lungs in action.

Telling the Body to Breathe

Christopher Reeve, the *Superman* actor, was paralysed in a horse-riding accident in 1995. He needed a mechanical ventilator to breathe. His portable machine weighed around 20 kg. It was smaller than a hospital ventilator, and let him live in his own home.

In 2003 he had surgery to implant a new electronic device into the chest. This tells the diaphragm (the main breathing muscle) to contract, so he may never again need his ventilator.

The film actor Christopher Reeve needed a machine to help him breathe after being hurt in a horse-riding accident.

23

Cleaning the Blood

It is very important that the right amount of water is kept inside the body and that the blood has the correct balance of chemicals. This is mainly the job of the kidneys, which get rid of unwanted water and chemicals by making urine.

When the kidneys are not working properly a person is said to be in renal (or kidney) failure.

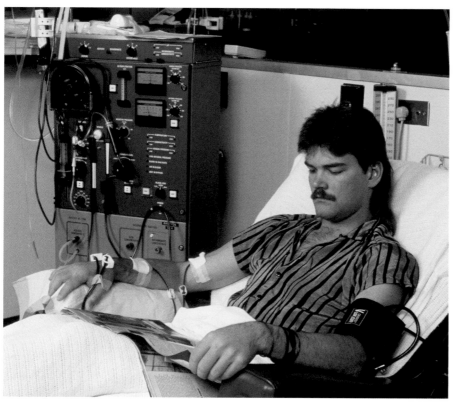

This man relaxes in hospital while his blood is cleaned by a dialysis machine. This can take several hours.

Dialysis Machines

Someone in renal failure needs the help of medical technology to keep them alive. In most cases this means that they will have to use an artificial kidney called a dialysis machine.

Dialysis machines may be used for patients who are staying in hospital, or they may be used in special clinics for people to visit.

During dialysis a tube is put into a vein in the patient's arm, and blood travels down the tube into the machine. Inside the machine the blood comes into contact with a very thin sheet, or membrane, which separates it from another liquid.

Waste chemicals from the blood pass through the membrane into the liquid which is eventually thrown away. The cleaned blood is returned to the body through another fine tube.

Looking Back

The First Artificial Kidney Sadly, before dialysis machines were invented, a person with kidney failure would die as waste substances built up in their blood.

The first artificial kidney was made in 1943 by Willem J. Kolff, a Dutch doctor who later worked in the United States. Many people are now being kept alive by modern versions of this machine.

Looking Forward

More Transplants One day it may be possible to make successful artificial kidneys which can be implanted within the body. It would probably be even more useful to make more kidneys available for transplant. Campaigners are working hard to tell people about the importance of carrying organ donor cards, saying that the carrier would like to give their kidneys if they die.

A surgeon prepares a donor kidney before implanting it into someone with kidney failure.

This process happens over and over again for around three to five hours, three times a week.

For some people, dialysis is only needed for a short time, then the kidneys recover. Others may get a new donor kidney, which means they no longer need dialysis. Many people, however, must use the dialysis machine for the rest of their lives.

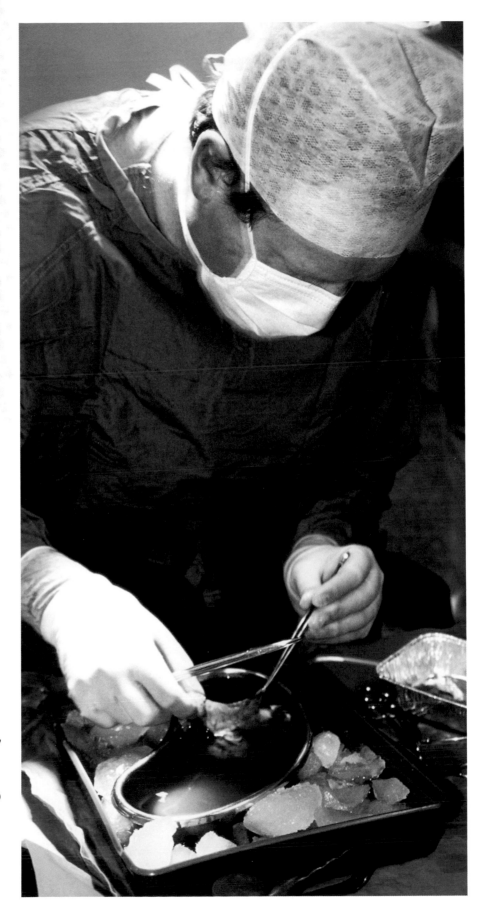

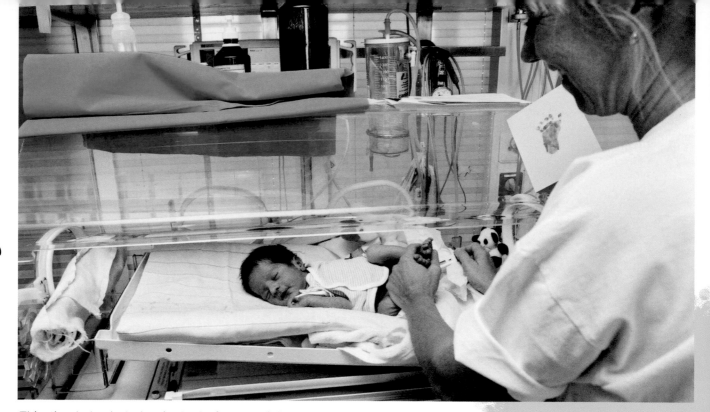

This tiny baby is being looked after carefully in a special cot called an incubator.

Some babies need special care after they are born, especially those who are born too early – known as premature babies. These babies may be very small and have problems with breathing and staying warm. They are also more likely to get an infection.

Incubators

Premature babies (as well as some with medical conditions) may need to be looked after in an incubator for a while. An incubator is a special box-like crib which has a heater to keep the baby warm.

Some incubators have a see-through lid which helps to keep the heat and moisture in. This lid usually has hand-sized holes so that carers can reach the baby without having to open the lid.

While the baby is inside the incubator, its breathing, temperature and heartbeat will be watched closely. Several kinds of wires and pads are gently attached to the baby to carry information back to electronic monitors around the incubator. If there is a problem an alarm will sound so the carers know right away.

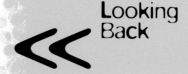

Looking Back

Babies on Show The first incubators were used in the late nineteenth century. At the Chicago World's Fair in 1933–4, premature babies in incubators were exhibited as an oddity which people queued to see!

It took many years for incubators to come into common use in our hospitals, but now they save many tiny lives.

Kelly's Story

Kelly was born in the summer of 2003, in the USA. She was tiny and quite poorly because she had arrived three months early. Kelly lived in an incubator for many weeks, being helped with her breathing and being treated with lots of different medicines.

At last, when she was three months old, her parents could take her home. Today she is fine, but without the incubator Kelly would probably have died.

Human Contact

We now know that it is very important for a baby to be touched and handled while it is in the incubator. The parents can stroke their babies and perhaps even hold them for a little while each day.

It may take days or weeks, but soon the baby should be strong enough to come out of the incubator and go home with its family.

Special instruments are being used by the doctor to help this baby start breathing.

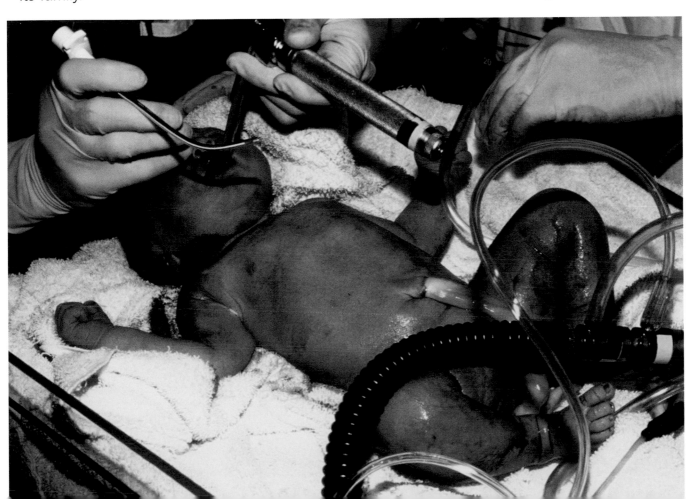

A laser is a device which makes a high-energy light beam. This beam of light can be used to cut human tissue like a tiny surgical knife. Laser beams are very narrow and can be controlled precisely. This is why they can be used to perform operations on delicate areas of the body.

Treating Cancer

Lasers are being used for treating the eyes, the skin, the feet and sometimes even the heart. One very important use for lasers is in treating women who are at risk of cervical cancer. In this condition, some of the cells found in the cervix, or neck of the womb, show signs of becoming cancerous.

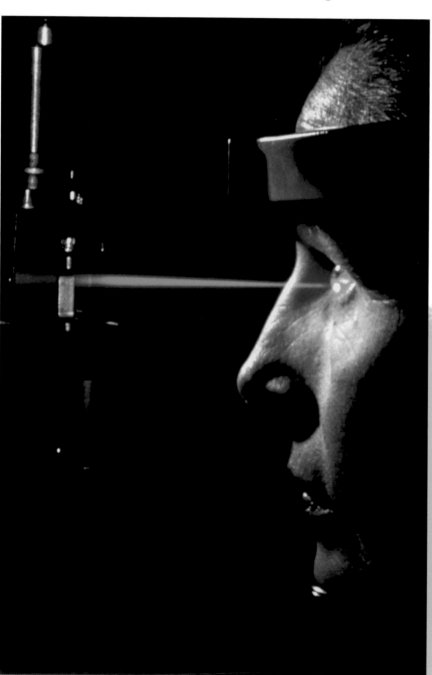

A laser can be used to destroy these cells before they can do any harm. It can do this without hurting the normal cells in that area.

This lady is having laser eye treatment. Her head must be held still in a brace to ensure the laser reaches the right part of the eye.

Looking Back

From Factory to Hospital

First developed in 1964, lasers were used in factories when precision cutting was important. When lasers were first used in medicine, around twenty years ago, doctors had to use adapted industrial lasers.

These days, modern medical lasers are designed just for use on human tissue. They have many special features which make them safer and more effective.

Laser Surgery for Eyes

Many people wear glasses or contact lenses to help them see. But some now choose to have laser eye surgery instead. This type of surgery changes the shape of the cornea (the see-through covering at the front of the eye) which then affects the eyesight.

One of the most popular methods is called LASIK. This involves cutting a tiny flap in the cornea with a minute surgical tool, and then using the laser to cut away some of the corneal tissue underneath.

Looking Forward

Cosmetic Surgery It is likely that lasers will be used more and more in many areas of medicine. Cosmetic surgery, which involves changing the way a person looks, is one area which is starting to make use of lasers. Laser surgery is already being done to remove some large birthmarks. It might also be able to make the skin look a little younger – which would be very popular with ageing film and TV stars!

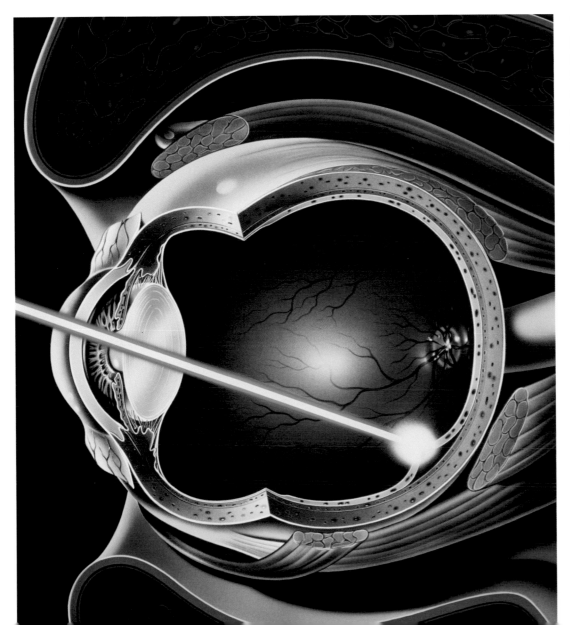

This cutaway picture of the eye shows where the beam of light goes during laser surgery on the back of the eye (the retina).

420 BCE Hippocrates begins the scientific study of medicine.

1451 CE Nicholas of Cusa invents spectacles (glasses) for short-sightedness.

1628 William Harvey first describes the way blood circulates (goes around and around) the body.

1763 Claudius Aymand is the first to successfully remove the appendix.

1816 René Laennec invents the stethoscope.

1842 Crawford Long performs the first surgical operation using anaesthesia (giving medicine to put the patient to sleep).

1859 Louis Pasteur suggests that some diseases may be caused by tiny living creatures.

1867 Joseph Lister shows that using disinfectants during operations reduces the number of infections afterwards.

1895 Wilhelm Roentgen discovers X-rays.

1899 The launch of a new painkiller called Aspirin.

1928 Alexander Fleming discovers penicillin, one of the first antibiotics (medicines which kill bacteria).

1933 Premature babies in incubators are displayed as an oddity at the Chicago World's Fair.

1943 The first artificial kidney is made by Willem Kolff.

1952 Paul Zoll develops one of the first artificial heart pacemakers.

1953 Surgeons perform the first successful open-heart surgery using a heart-lung machine, at Jefferson Medical College in Philadelphia, USA.

1953 Watson and Crick solved the puzzle of the structure of DNA, the chemical which carries genetic information.

1953 Jonas Salk successfully tests a new polio vaccine.

1954 The first successful human organ transplant is performed. A kidney taken from one identical twin is given to the other.

1957 Willem Kolff tests his artificial heart in animals.

1959 Wilson Greatbach keeps one of his patients alive for eighteen months with his artificial pacemaker.

1964 Lasers are developed for use in industry.

1967 Christiaan Barnard performs the first successful heart transplant.

1973 Paul Christian Lauterbur publishes the first MRI (magnetic resonance imaging) body scan. This type of scanning soon becomes widely used.

1978 The first test-tube baby is born.

1982 Barney Clark survives 112 days with an artificial heart called the Jarvik 7.

1987 The first heart-lung transplant is performed.

1990 The Human Genome Project is launched. This is a study to find all the genes in the human body.

2000 The Human Genome Project delivers the first draft of the complete genetic information for the human body.

birthmark A harmless red or brown mark on the skin which is there at birth.

cancer A serious illness which often includes the growth of lumps (tumours) somewhere in the body.

carbon fibre A strong and light man-made material.

cardiopulmonary bypass machine A machine which does the work of the heart and lungs. Also called a heart-lung machine.

cervix The neck, or lower opening, of the womb (the female organ which holds a growing baby).

cochlea The snail-shaped organ which lies in the inner ear. It turns sound waves into electrical signals to send to the brain.

cornea The see-through part of the surface of the eyeball, which covers the coloured iris and the black pupil.

defibrillator A machine which gives an electric shock to the heart to make it beat properly.

diagnosis The identification of a person's illness.

dialysis using a machine to do the work of the kidney. Dialysis machines get rid of unwanted liquid and chemicals from the blood.

donor Someone who gives a part of their body after they die to help someone else.

donor cards A card carried by someone to say they wish to give a part of their body after they die to help someone else.

echocardiogram An ultrasound scan of the heart.

endoscope A long bendy tube with a camera at the end. It is used for looking deep inside the body.

gallbladder A small organ in the tummy which makes a liquid needed to break down food.

gullet The tube which joins the mouth to the stomach. Also called the oesophagus.

hearing aid A small electronic device which helps someone to hear better.

heart transplant When someone is given a new heart because their own doesn't work anymore.

heart-lung machine A machine which does the work of the heart and lungs (also called a cardiopulmonary bypass machine)

implanted When a device is implanted a surgeon cuts opens the body, fixes the device inside, then sews the cut up.

incubator A special crib-like machine that a poorly, newborn baby can be put inside to keep it safe and warm.

intestine also called the gut, this is the long tube which food travels along inside the body.

iron lung A large ventilator which completely encloses a person from the neck down.

Kevlar A very strong man-made material used in some artificial limbs, and bullet-proof vests!

keyhole surgery Surgical operations performed through tiny cuts, with the surgeon using an endoscope to see what he or she is doing.

left ventricular assist device (LVAD) A small electronic device which is implanted in the heart to help it do its work.

murmur An abnormal sound made by the heart. It can be heard with a stethoscope.

pacemaker Either the part of the heart which tells the rest of the heart muscle when to beat, or a man-made electronic device which does the same job.

paralysed If someone is paralysed they can no longer move a part of their body.

polio A serious illness caused by a virus. It can make someone paralysed (unable to move parts of their body).

premature A baby is premature if it is born weeks or months too early.

prosthesis Something artificial (man-made) which replaces a part of the body

renal To do with the kidneys.

surgical wound A cut made in the skin by a surgeon when a person is asleep during an operation

titanium A very strong and light metal.

ultrasound Sound waves which can be used to look inside the body.

urine The water passed out when going to the toilet.

vaccine A medicine or jab which is given to stop a person getting an infection in the future.

ventilator A machine which pushes air into the lungs to help a person who cannot breathe for themselves.

virtual Not real. A virtual image seems real but is actually made by a computer.

X-rays Rays that can't be seen by our eyes but can be used to take pictures of the inside of the body.

Further Information

Further Reading

Genes and DNA by Richard Walker (Kingfisher Publications, 2003)
How Things Work by John Farndon (Miles Kelly Science Library, 2004)
How Your Body Works by Judy Hindley and C. J. Rawson (Usborne Publishing, 1995)
The Usborne Internet-Linked Complete Book of the Human Body by Anna Claybourne (Usborne Publishing, 2003)
Incredible Body by Stephen Biesty and Richard Platt (illustrator) (Dorling Kindersley, 1998)
Action Pack: Human Body (Dorling Kindersley, 2003)

CD-ROMs

The Ultimate Human Body 2.0 (Dorling Kindersley)
Become a Human Body Explorer (Dorling Kindersley)
Encyclopaedia Britannica: Human Body (Focus Multimedia)

Websites

http://www.howstuffworks.com
Covers several topics in medical technology, including X-rays and various types of scanners.

http://www.bbc.co.uk/science/humanbody/
A BBC website that looks at the human body and mind.

http://www.innerbody.com/
An exploration of the human anatomy, including animation, graphics and descriptive links.

http://www.kidshealth.org/kid/body/mybody.html
Information and health tips for every part of the body.

http://yucky.kids.discovery.com/
Full of gross, yucky – as well as cool – facts about the body.

Index